12 Months of

Divine Love:

Poetry Edition

Will Brown

JANUARY

This Covenant

Thank you my love for the fortitude to
See a new year
Filled with great opportunities.
Come closer and embellish me
While we endure the winds that
Blow around us. I need to feel the Warmth of your embrace.
Complete me as we unite and
Become one. You are my sanctuary.
The place where I find rest, peace,
Joy and happiness.
Although the chill from the cold permeates
The air, even still your love illuminates and fills
My temple. No one can enter, because Of the covenant we have in each other.
You are irresistible, irreplaceable and
We have been ordained to be together.
Inevitably we are destiny! The agape
Love of God has found its place within us.
Our souls have been predestined for this moment, In this journey called romance.
Although the winter has come to bring the storms
Of triumph, we have been equipped with the fruits
Of the spirit, to withstand all opposition.
Together we are unstoppable. We are more Than conquers. We are one!
As I lay in your gardens, let me fertilize your soil And pour into you the oil of joy.
Let me wrap you in garments of praise
And enjoy the splendor of your beauty.
Let me adore the fragrance of your hair.
My sword will always protect you. My shield will Withstand the arrows that attack at noonday.
I'll stand and watch over your gates. I'll prevent
Thieves from stealing your fine linens and treasure.
Nothing can defy us because we are covenant

February

Our Love

Love is in the air! Like a dove souring
Throughout the earth
It's waiting to descend.
I open up my palace doors
For the arrival of such a time As this.
For this is a unique moment In time as our hearts
Entwine with one another.
My soul is willing and waiting
To become one with yours.
Our eyes are set as an Eagle
In flight lurking its prey.
Our arms are open wide to receive
Only the best of what God has to offer.
The stars of universe affirm our union
With it's illumination of bright
Lights from heavens throne.
The moon even gives her contribution
By adorning our courtship like a giant pearl
Announcing the midnight.
And when love has found its place
On our mantle,
The Sun shall shine bright in the
Morning hours, to endorse the paradise
That has been discovered between us.
Yes love is here my king, my queen and
Has established its territory.
Now we can reign and rule
As a royal priesthood
A holy nation acceptable onto
The most high God, For our divine purpose
To share love, give love and love one another.

March
Lasting Memories

I've never met anyone as beautiful as you
The moment I looked into your eyes and embraced
Your smile my soul ignited for the first time
The moment you walked into my life
The world stopped spinning just so that
You could get on
I knew at that instance that I'd never be the same
Thank you my love for knocking on heavens door
So many days I prayed for someone like you
Yes unique and unafraid of being vulnerable
Full of laughter and character yet bold enough to stand
On your own
Someone humble and passionate and without
A price
Because of that my love, you are priceless
You are my air
As the lightning flashes and the earth winds blows
I wait to bask in your sensitivity and to endure
The sweet smell of your presence
There is no greater love than yours because
You are love, you are strength, you are whole
Thank you for allowing me to open a gift
Like you
And experience what it means to finally
See God's glory made for me.

April
Enduring The Rain

I offer my cup in the celebration
Of our success
Thank you for bringing out the best
In me
For releasing me from all of
My fears
And helping me to identify the
Greatness within me
The drying of my tears and of all The loneliness
My heart is restored from all the
Brokenness
Because you believe in me
Thank you for the gift of you
Full of unlimited rain and pleasure
Your endless drops of unconditional love
Has cleansed me from all
My mistakes and pain I empty everything in my cup
To fill yours and celebrate you So prepare to receive all that I have
And all that I am
Like the fallen showers that April brings
Here's to new beginnings of God's new thing
Let's together fill our glass
With new wine
As the spring air brings forth new joy
Surrounded by the security we've created
Drink the free flowing wine from my hand picked vines
That have been prepare for us
As we continue to prosper.

May

A New Season

We made it my dear
Yes we made it just you and I
I feel the warmth of my smile
As I embellish the calm in your eyes
I yearn for your touch
As you wipe away the tears of joy
That cannot be ignored
As the birds chirp in the morning hour
Alerting the sun to break
We rise
No one believed we could make it
Now I stand here glazing at your essence
Your countenance your beauty
And all that you are
From the very start I knew you were the
Perfect one for me
Strong enough for me bold enough for me
Able to bring out the best in me
God has bless us for this moment
To reflect on His excellence in us
Yes a new season filled with honor accolades
And oh how can we forget not to mention
All of our haters who doubted our success
But here we are just you and me and the strength of God
Hold me tighter love me more and whatever you do
Don't ever let me go because I'm am nothing without you
Or you without me because we are one we are we
And there could be no other.

Summer Love

June
Agape Madness

My sweetness from heaven
The one that I adore
For your love I'll swim across the
Deepest rivers
Even search the oceans Shores
I possess the keys to unlock all
Your doors
To share your thoughts and visions
Where your secrets lie
So innocent yet sublime
You're the essence of the finest
Flower on earth
Hidden in fields and enduring
The summers heat
Your skin and statue is more beautiful and
Radiate than the tallest cedars From Lebanon
Because I have you by my side
I can fly higher than any Eagle
Or greatest plane roaring through The skies
We can soar up and down and across
Horizons yet to be discovered
Oh how good it feels to be two miles
From heaven
The worst thing that can happen
Is for my feet to touch the ground
Nevertheless I know you will descend With me
I'll follow you like a dove going back to
It's nest To share the love of it's mate and
Manifest the glory of the
Summer madness

July

Body Soul and Spirit

I love you for all the times You never left me side
For every tear you've wiped From my eyes
So many times you looked inside my heart
And made me see
That only the best resides in me
No matter how many wrongs
That I tried to hide
You always gave me your smile
Instead of vain arrogance and pride
You gave me strength to believe
Thank you for really loving me
Every time it seems as if
I'm about to fall
You're always there to pick me up
To help me stand tall
You are my inspiration my everything To me
This world is a better place because of you
You bring me unspeakable joy
Even lift me up when I cannot reach
When I embrace your touch
I hear the pulse of your heartbeat
As the sweat rolls down my face From your body heat
You've made my life complete
My sunshine in the mist of the clouds My cool in the shade
My drink that quenches my thirst
Yes it's the taste of your sugar cane Lips
On a hot summers day I burn for your touch
You're the sweetest thing
I've ever known
Thank you for being so good to me
You are my body heat

August
In Too Deep

You're all that I've ever Known
Come to me and let us share
Kisses in the dark
While dancing 360 degrees
In the moon light
Exchanging our souls
As we our lips meet
For the ultimate pleasure
Tasting love so sweet
The experiences of what happiness
Really is and not what someone else
Thinks it should be You're the sound of the E note that
Turns into our symphony
There are no greater riches
Than the dirt I hold
In my hands from the spirit of your soil
We've build trust and understanding
That rush in like waves
To greet the shores of life's Stormy seas
And still waters begins to fill
The lakes of my heart
You are my hidden treasure
Discovered in a field
Thank you for this exchange
Of life and dreams
We've survived through it all
And I salute to you with clear
Blue skies As I smile while looking
Into your eyes
I realize I'm not going anywhere
Without you because I'm in too deep

September

My Destiny

Another season has presented
Us the best of life Leaves fall from
The trees Even the sun's going
Down earlier
Leaving days shorter
Than the one before
While cool winds begin
To fill the air With gentle breezes
Permeating your scent
In the air Your are here
So amazing and even
Greater than I could
Have ever imagined
How selfish of me to ask
For more More of what God has Given me
Yes you're the gift that's
Sweeter than sweet
More adorable than yesterday
A force unstoppable And empowered by
The most high, His grace continually
Shines on us to rule and reign
And everything that we do Shall prosper
Even our seed shall bring Good fruit and reap the
Inheritance of what we've created
Because we are blessed
Let me look into your eyes
And gaze into your glamour
My love I close my eyes to embrace
The honey that lingers on your lips
As we embrace the tomorrow
Still to come

October

Sensational

Each step I take draws me
Closer to you
Willingly I hear your spirit
Calling me louder and louder
Like a light in darkness
Your smile guilds me to your
Garden of treasure like a divine compass
As I stand here looking into your eyes
I see visions of divine purpose sparkling
Like shooting stars
Sending me sublime messages that you
Are God's gift
Your lips dripping like raw Brown sugar
Your skin glistening black coal
From the earths core
In amazement I watch you transform
Into a fine diamond hidden for
Such a time as this Your soul cries out to me
I am God's gift
As I reach out to grab your soul
And wrap our arms around
Each other we become one
The heavens open and create
The sanctuary God has already prepared
For us because we are destiny
Ordained before the foundations of time
Filled with the ordinates of authority
Power, rulership and dominion.
Life belongs to us to possess because God has
Already blessed us with his spirit.
We are Destiny

November

You

I honor you for being so precious
I've watched you grow from glory
To glory
I bow at your feet for being the man that you are
God has turned you into a king
For my pleasure I
He trusted you enough to know
That you would surpass the strategies
Of the adversary
And that your tomorrow
Would be greater than your today
Yes your later days have become greater
Than your former days
I bless you for allowing me to journey with you
To see God's great work revealed
I praise you for choosing me as
Your perfect soul mate
Praying over you and for you
When we had nothing
And now we have everything
Because of you I believe the unbelievable
Think the unthinkable because you are
God's example of greatness and authority
You are marvelous you are treasure
You are wonderful you are excellence
You are me and I am you
We are one

December
Legacy

Last night we prayed
Last night we made love
Last night we celebrated
The magnificence's of God's mercy
Yes we were chosen for this journey
We have broken down the doors
And taken back what the enemy
Has stolen for centuries
Now we can restore the perfect order
Of our families inheritance that
Can now be shared for generations
And generations to come
Now we can dream dreams
Now we can own the fat of the land
Now we can distribute the gold and silver
Now we can open and own banks
Now we can experience butlers and maidservants
This is our time to establish a good work
We have been chosen as God's best
With unlimited favor
For His great purpose
Trendsetters and kingdom examples
On the earth to bring rulership and legacy

12 MONTHS OF DIVINE LOVE: POETRY COLLECTION

Printed in the United States of America

ISBN-13:978-0692614716
ISBN-10:0692614710

Printed by Createspace 2016
Published by BlaqRayn Publishing Plus 2016